Princess Plates:
Enchanting Recipes Fit for Royalty

Marlow Miller

Introduction

Welcome to the magical world of *Princess Plates: Enchanting Recipes Fit for Royalty!*

Get ready to embark on a delicious journey filled with giggles, tasty treats, and kitchen adventures. In this cookbook designed just for little chefs, we've gathered the yummiest recipes for breakfast, lunch, dinner, snacks, and desserts, turning ordinary meals into extraordinary moments. Join us as we explore the wonders of the kitchen together, creating memories that will last a lifetime!

🔍 Dive into exciting breakfast creations!
🥪 Craft scrumptious lunchtime masterpieces!
🍕 Explore dinner delights that are both tasty and fun!
🍿 Snack attacks have never been this exciting!
🍰 Conclude your culinary day with delightful desserts!

Let the laughter and learning begin as we mix, stir, and bake our way to a world of flavor. *Princess Plates: Enchanting Recipes Fit for Royalty* is not just a cookbook; it's a recipe for joy, bonding, and discovery. Happy cooking, little chefs!

Table of Contents

How do you make a tissue dance?

You put a little boogie in it!

Why did the cookie go to
the doctor?

It was feeling crumbly.

BREAKFAST

Sunshine Pancakes

Preparation Time:
10 minutes

Cooking Time:
15 minutes

Servings:
2

Ingredients:

- 1 cup Pancake Mix
- 1 cup Milk
- 2-3 Strawberries sliced
- 2 Blueberries
- 5-6 Chocolate Chips

Instructions:

1. Mix pancake mix and milk until smooth.
2. Heat a griddle or pan over medium heat.
3. Pour small amounts of batter onto the griddle to form sun shapes.
4. Cook until bubbles form, then flip and cook the other side.
5. Place pancake in the middle of plate.
6. Place Strawberries slices as sunrays.
7. Use blueberries for sun eyes and chocolate chips for smile.

Nutrition facts:
(per serving)

- Calories: 180cals
- Carbs: 13g
- Protein: 5g
- Fat: 7g

Why don't eggs tell each other secrets?

Because they might crack up!

Fruity Butterfly Toast

Preparation Time:
8 minutes

Cooking Time:
0 minutes

Servings:
1

Ingredients:

- 1 slice Whole Wheat Bread
- 1 tablespoon Peanut Butter or Nut Butter
- 1 Strawberry
- 1 Banana
- Handful of Raisins

Instructions:

1. Toast the bread slices.
2. Arrange the toast into butterfly wings.
3. Spread peanut butter or nut butter on the wings.
4. Arrange strawberry and banana slices on wings.
5. Add banana for the body.
6. Use raisins for the eyes.

Nutrition facts:
(per serving)

Calories: 150cals
Carbs: 25g
Protein: 4g
Fat: 7g

Why did the turtle cross the road?

To get to the shell station!

Caterpillar Fruit Skewers

Preparation Time:
15 minutes

Cooking Time:
0 minutes

Servings:
4

Ingredients:

- 16 Grapes
- 4 Strawberries
- 8 Edible eyes
- 1 teaspoon Cream Cheese or Greek Yogurt
- 4 long Toothpicks or small Skewers

Nutrition facts:
(per serving)

» Calories: 80cals
» Carbs: 14g
» Protein: 1g
» Fat: 1g

Instructions:

1. Wash and prepare the fruit.
2. Thread grapes onto skewers as the body and add strawberry on the top to create a caterpillar face.
3. Place edible eyes on strawberries with the cream cheese or Greek yogurt.
4. Enjoy.

8

Owl Face Oatmeal

Preparation Time: 15 minutes

Cooking Time: 10 minutes

Servings: 3

Ingredients:

- 1 cup Oatmeal
- 2 cups Milk
- 7 Almonds
- 2 Kiwi slices
- 2 Strawberry slice
- 2 Blueberries
- 1 teaspoon Yogurt

Nutrition facts:
(per serving)

Calories: 220cals
Carbs: 20g
Protein: 6g
Fat: 4g

Instructions:

1. Cook oatmeal according to package instructions using milk.
2. Place oatmeal in the bowl.
3. Place kiwi slices, blueberries, yogurt on top to resemble eyes and almonds for eyelashes and nose.
4. You can optionally place strawberry slices for cheeks.

What do you call a snowman with a six-pack?

An abdominal snowman!

Teddy Bear Toast

Preparation Time:
5 minutes

Cooking Time:
0 minutes

Servings:
3

Ingredients:

- 3 Slices Whole Grain Bread
- 1 tablespoon Peanut Butter or any Nut Butter
- 1 Banana, sliced
- Handful of Blueberries

Instructions:

1. Toast the bread slices.
2. Spread peanut butter or nut butter on the toast.
3. Arrange banana slice to create teddy bear ears and nose.
4. Place blueberries for the eyes and nose.

Nutrition facts:
(per serving)
- Calories: 210cals
- Carbs: 27g
- Protein: 6g
- Fat: 4g

Wise Owl Fruity Toast

Preparation Time: 15 minutes

Cooking Time: 2 minutes

Servings: 1

Ingredients:

- 1 English Muffin , sliced
- 2 tablespoons peanut butter or nut butter
- 1 Banana, sliced
- 2 Strawberries, simply sliced
- Handful of Blueberries

Nutrition facts:
(per serving)
Calories: 90cals
Carbs: 15g
Protein: 3g
Fat: 6g

Instructions:

1. Toast the English muffin until just lightly browning.
2. Spread the toasted muffin halves with peanut butter or nut butter.
3. Arrange banana slices and blueberries for eyes, strawberry slices for ears, and cut-up strawberry pieces for owl beak.
4. Spread some blueberries on the plate and your toasted muffins will now look like little owls!

Why did the teddy bear say no to dessert?

Because it was already stuffed!

Ice Cream Cone Pancakes

Preparation Time: 10 minutes

Cooking Time: 15 minutes

Servings: 2

Ingredients:

- 1 cup Pancake Mix
- 1 cup Milk
- 2 Bananas, sliced
- Sprinkles or Candies (optional)
- Honey or Maple Syrup (optional)

Nutrition facts:
(per serving)

- » Calories: 200cals
- » Carbs: 35g
- » Protein: 6g
- » Fat: 8g

Instructions:

1. Follow the instructions on the ready-made pancake mix to prepare the batter.
2. Heat a griddle or non-stick skillet over medium heat.
3. Pour the pancake batter onto the griddle in the shape of a cone. Cook according to the package instructions until golden brown.
4. Add sprinkles or candies.
5. Drizzle or dip cone and fruit with honey or maple syrup.

Why did the banana go to the doctor?

Because it wasn't peeling well!

Banana Split Parfait

Preparation Time:
10 minutes

Cooking Time:
0 minutes

Servings:
1

Ingredients:

- 1 Banana, sliced
- 1 cup Vanilla Yogurt
- 2 tablespoons Strawberry Jam or a handful of Fresh Strawberries, sliced
- Whipped Cream (as desired)
- Rainbow Sprinkles (optional)
- Maraschino Cherries (optional)

Nutrition facts:
(per serving)

Calories: 250cals
Carbs: 33g
Protein: 12g
Fat: 10g

Instructions:

1. In a bowl, start by placing a layer of sliced bananas at the bottom.
2. Spoon a layer of vanilla yogurt over the bananas.
3. Spoon a layer of strawberry jam or add sliced fresh strawberries on top.
4. Finish off the parfait by adding a generous dollop of whipped cream on top.
5. Optionally, add rainbow sprinkles for a colorful touch.
6. Top with a maraschino cherry for an extra fun element.
7. Present the Banana Split Parfait to the kids and enjoy this delightful and tasty treat!

13

Rainbow Fruit Kabob

 **Preparation Time:** 15 minutes

 Cooking Time: 0 minutes

 Servings: 2

Ingredients:

- ½ cup Pineapple Chunks
- ½ cup Cherries
- ½ cup Orange
- ½ cup Grapes
- ½ cup Blueberries
- ½ cup Strawberries, halved
- Skewers, or Long Toothpicks

Nutrition facts:
(per serving)

- Calories: 100cals
- Carbs: 25g
- Protein: 1g
- Fat: 1g

Instructions:

1. Thread the fruits onto skewers in the following rainbow order: orange, pineapple, blueberries, cherries, grapes and strawberries.
2. Repeat until the skewer is filled with colorful fruit.
3. Serve the rainbow fruit kabobs on a plate.

What do you call a fish wearing a bowtie?

Sofishticated!

14

Teddy Bear Pancake

Preparation Time:
10 minutes

Cooking Time:
5 minutes

Servings:
2

Ingredients:

- Pancake Mix (store-bought or homemade)
- 3 Berries (for eyes and nose)
- 3 Banana slices (for ears)
- Sliced Strawberries (for bow tie)

Instructions:

1. Follow the instructions on the pancake mix box or prepare a simple pancake batter.
2. Pour small circles for the body and larger circles for the head on a griddle or skillet.
3. Cook until bubbles appear on the surface, then flip and cook until golden brown. Place the cooked pancakes on a plate.
4. Add Berries for eyes and a nose.
5. Use sliced strawberries or bananas for ears.

Nutrition facts:
(per serving)

Calories: 290cals
Carbs: 31g
Protein: 7g
Fat: 10g

What do you call a bear with no teeth?

A gummy bear!

What kind of tree fits in your hand?

A palm tree!

Why did the bicycle fall over?

Because it was two-tired!

16

LUNCH

Birdie Kix

Preparation Time:
20 minutes

Cooking Time:
0 minutes

Servings:
1

Ingredients:

- 1 round slice of Pineapple
- 1 Baby Carrot
- 2 Black Currants
- Handful of Pretzel Sticks
- Handful of Berry or Berry Kix Cereal

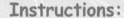

Nutrition facts:
(per serving)
» Calories: 280cals
» Carbs: 30g
» Protein: 7g
» Fat: 3g

Instructions:

1. Grab a plate and place your round slice of pineapple in the center. Place some pretzel twists around the bottom of the plate to resemble a bird's nest.
2. Using your knife (please supervise children if allowing them to slice), slice your baby carrot into 2 thin rounds. Carefully slice 2 tiny triangles from the bottoms of those rounds. Place these on the bird for the feet.
3. Next, slice another round off your carrot and cut it into a triangle. Place this triangle on your bird for the nose. Finally, slice 3 thin strips off the remaining baby carrot. Stick these on top of the birdie for the top feathers.
4. Take your 2 black currants and place them on the birdie for the eyes.
5. Lastly, grab a handful of Berry Berry Kix cereal and put some in the empty spaces in your nest.

Rainbow Veggie Wraps

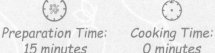

Preparation Time: 15 minutes

Cooking Time: 0 minutes

Servings: 4

Ingredients:

- 4 Large Tortillas
- ½ cup Red Bell Pepper, thinly sliced
- 1 cup Orange Carrots, sliced
- 1 cup Hummus
- ½ cup Corns
- ½ cup Green Beans
- ½ Purple Cabbage, thinly sliced

Nutrition facts:
(per serving)

Calories: 320cals
Carbs: 24g
Protein: 3g
Fat: 1g

Instructions:

1. Spread ¼ cup of hummus evenly on each tortilla.
2. Arrange the sliced veggies in rainbow order on top of the hummus-covered tortilla.
3. Add a layer of bell pepper carrots, corn, green beans and purple cabbage.
4. Carefully roll up each tortilla to form a wrap.
5. Slice each wrap into smaller portions for easy serving.

How do you organize a space party?

You planet!

Hot Air Balloon Waffle

Preparation Time:
15 minutes

Cooking Time:
5 minutes

Servings:
4

Ingredients:

- 1 Gluten Free Waffle
- 2 Strawberries, sliced
- ½ Cantaloupe, sliced
- 6 -7 Pineapple Chunks
- 2 Kiwi, sliced
- 1 Banana, sliced
- Handful of Blueberries
- 1 Mini Waffle

Nutrition facts:
(per serving)

» Calories: 80cals
» Carbs: 11g
» Protein: 7g
» Fat: 9g

Instructions:

1. Toast waffles per packaging instructions.
2. Place one waffle in the center of your plate to create the base of the balloon. You can create the basket with a second waffle or with a Mini Waffle.
3. Cut the strawberries, cantaloupe, pineapple and kiwi into small chunks and arrange them on the waffle to create alliterating rows of color.
4. Connect the basket to the balloon with a string of blueberries on each side.
5. Arranged banana slices to create clouds around your Hot Air Balloon Waffles.

What's a vampire's favorite fruit?

A blood orange!

Bunny Sandwiches

Preparation Time: 15 minutes

Cooking Time: 0 minutes

Servings: 2

Ingredients:

- 4 slices of Bread
- ½ pound Deli Turkey or Ham
- 4 Cheese slices
- 1 Carrot, thinly sliced
- 3 Black Olives (for eyes & nose)
- Edible Eyes (Optional)

Nutrition facts:
(per serving)

Calories: 240cals
Carbs: 30g
Protein: 10g
Fat: 9g

Instructions:

1. Lay out 2 slices of bread on a flat surface.
2. Place an equal amount of deli turkey or ham on each slice.
3. Add a cheese slice on top of the meat.
4. Top each sandwich with another slice of bread.
5. Using a bunny-shaped cookie cutter, or cut each sandwich into a bunny shape.
6. Cut cheese into a bunny face and ears, place it on the bread.
7. Add carrot slices for whiskers, and olives for eyes & nose (optional: edible eyes).

Why did the math book look sad?

Because it had too many problems.

Banana Heaven

Preparation Time:
10 minutes

Cooking Time:
0 minutes

Servings:
2

Ingredients:

- 2 Bananas, cut in half longwise
- 6 Chocolates Chunks
- 4 Strawberries slice
- 8 – 9 Blueberries
- 8 – 9 Raspberries
- 2 tablespoons Peanut Butter or any Nut Butter

Instructions:

1. Cut 2 bananas in half longwise and place them on a plate.
2. Spread peanut butter or nut butter on all 4 bananas and place chocolate, strawberry, blueberry and raspberry.
3. Enjoy.

Nutrition facts:
(per serving)

- Calories: 100cals
- Carbs: 9g
- Protein: 12g
- Fat: 14g

What do you call a sleeping bull?

A bulldozer!

Marshmellow and Fruit Skewers

Preparation Time: 15 minutes

Cooking Time: 0 minutes

Servings: 4

Ingredients:

- 1 Pack Marshmallow
- $\frac{1}{4}$ cup Peanut Butter or Nut Butter
- 8 Strawberries or 2 Bananas sliced into chunks
- Cream
- Toothpicks or Skewers

Instructions:

1. Spread peanut butter or nut butter on one end of marshmallow, for fruit to stick.
2. Add marshmallow and strawberry (or banana chunk) with peanut butter or nut butter in between on skewer.
3. Add cream dots on strawberry for complete look.
4. Enjoy

Nutrition facts: (per serving)
Calories: 80cals
Carbs: 5g
Protein: 2g
Fat: 5g

What do you get when you cross a snowman and a vampire?

Frostbite!

Dinosaur Sandwiches

Preparation Time: 15 minutes

Cooking Time: 0 minutes

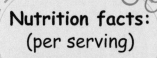
Servings: 4

Ingredients:

- 8 Slices of Bread
- 1 cup Cream Cheese
- ½ pound Deli Turkey or Ham
- 1 cup Lettuce, shredded

Instructions:

1. Lay out 4 slices of bread on a flat surface.
2. Spread approximately ¼ cup of cream cheese evenly on each slice of bread.
3. Add an equal amount of deli turkey or ham on top of the cream cheese.
4. Sprinkle shredded lettuce over the meat.
5. Top each sandwich with another slice of bread.
6. Use a dinosaur-shaped cookie cutter to create fun dinosaur-shaped sandwiches.

Nutrition facts:
(per serving)

» Calories: 150cals
» Carbs: 5g
» Protein: 5g
» Fat: 10g

Granola Apple Sandwiches

Ingredients:

- 1 Apple, cored and sliced horizontally
- 1 tablespoon Peanut Butter or Nut Butter
- Granola or Raisins (Optional)

Instructions:

1. Spread peanut butter or nut butter on one side of each apple slice.
2. Sprinkle granola or raisins on the peanut butter or nut butter side of one slice.
3. Top with another apple slice to create a sandwich.

Nutrition facts:
(per serving)

Calories: 70cals
Carbs: 8g
Protein: 4g
Fat: 3g

Banana and Nut Butter Wrap

Preparation Time: 10 minutes

Cooking Time: 0 minutes

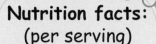

Servings: 6

Ingredients:

- 1 Whole Wheat Tortilla
- 2 tablespoons Peanut Butter or Nut Butter
- 1 Banana, sliced
- Chocolate Chips (Optional)

Instructions:

1. Spread almond butter or peanut butter or nut butter on a whole wheat tortilla.
2. Place banana slices on one half of the tortilla.
3. Sprinkle chocolate chips on it.
4. Fold or roll the tortilla in half to create a wrap.

Nutrition facts:
(per serving)

- Calories: 250cals
- Carbs: 24g
- Protein: 11g
- Fat: 12g

Fun Fruit Train

 Preparation Time:
10 minutes

 Cooking Time:
0 minutes

Servings:
1

Ingredients:

- ½ Watermelon
- 2 Bananas, sliced
- 2 Blueberries
- 1 Apple slice
- 1 Raspberry
- 1 Pineapple Chunk
- 1 teaspoon Yogurt
- 10 -12 Toothpicks

Nutrition facts:
(per serving)
Calories: 90cals
Carbs: 8g
Protein: 3g
Fat: 4g

Instructions:

1. Cut the water melon into two rectangles, one smaller than the other.
2. Cut 1 banana in half, slice the other banana into 8 slices.
3. Stack watermelon pieces
4. Stack banana halves, pineapple and raspberry on top using toothpicks
5. Attached banana slices with toothpicks for wheels and caboose top.
6. Attach apple slice and blueberries with yogurt for headlights.

What do you get when you cross a cat with a dark cloud?

A scaredy-cat!

How does a penguin build its house?

Igloos it together!

DINNER

Kite Sandwich

Preparation Time:
15 minutes

Cooking Time:
0 minutes

Servings:
1

Ingredients:

- 1 slice of Bread
- 1 slice of Cheese
- 6 Raspberries
- 5-6 pieces of Popcorn
- 1 Carrot Stick

Instructions:

1. Start by cutting a slice of bread into a square, either freehand or using a cookie cutter.
2. Trim a slice of cheese to the same size, and then quarter it diagonally.
3. Place two quarters of cheese on top of the bread, as shown. (You can add a little mayo, if desired.)
4. Use a sharp knife to trim a carrot stick into a thin kite tail.
5. Arrange raspberries along the sides of it.
6. Add popcorn as clouds.

Nutrition facts:
(per serving)

» Calories: 90cals
» Carbs: 7g
» Protein: 4g
» Fat: 9g

What did one wall say to the other wall?

"I'll meet you at the corner!"

Traffic Light Sandwiches

Preparation Time: 10 minutes

Cooking Time: 0 minutes

Servings: 4

Ingredients:

- 8 slices Whole meal Sandwich Bread, crusts removed
- 1/3 cup Corn Relish
- 4 slices Cheese
- 4 Red Cherry Tomatoes, sliced in half
- 4 Yellow Cherry Tomatoes, sliced in half
- 4 Lettuce Leaves

**Nutrition facts:
(per serving)**
Calories: 250cals
Carbs: 32g
Protein: 12g
Fat: 11g

Instructions:

1. Place half the bread slices on a flat surface. Spread with relish. Top with cheese.
2. Place tomato slices on cheese for the traffic lights.
3. Place folded, or small, lettuce leaf along bottom on cheese.
4. Using a 1.5cm round cutter, cut 2 rows of 3 circles from remaining bread, to form 2 sets of traffic lights.
5. Place bread over filling.
6. Cut each sandwich in half to make 2 traffic lights.
7. Serve.

What did the ocean say to the shore?

Nothing, it just waved!

Hot Dog Bun Car

Preparation Time: 15 minutes

Cooking Time: 0 minutes

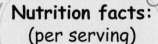

Servings: 4

Ingredients:

- 4 Hot Dog Buns
- 4 Hot Dogs
- 4 Cheese slices
- 10 Cherry Tomatoes, sliced in half
- 16 Cucumber slices
- Ketchup, Mustard and Mayo (Optional)

Nutrition facts:
(per serving)
- Calories: 250cals
- Carbs: 30g
- Protein: 12g
- Fat: 10g

Instructions:

1. Cook the hot dogs according to the package instructions.
2. Place a hot dog inside each bun.
3. Cut a slice of cheese into a triangular shape to resemble the car's roof.
4. Attach cucumbers and tomato slices to sides with toothpicks or mayo for wheels.
5. Add tomato slices on top of hot dog for car dome.
6. Use ketchup, mustard, or mayo for fun details.
7. Remove toothpicks before eating.
8. Arrange cars on a plate and enjoy.

Greek Yogurt Parfait

Preparation Time: 15 minutes

Cooking Time: 0 minutes

Servings: 1

Ingredients:

- 1 cup Greek Yogurt
- ½ cup Granola
- ½ cup Mixed Berries (Strawberries, Blueberries)
- Honey (optional)

Instructions:

1. In a cup or bowl, layer ½ cup of Greek yogurt, ¼ cup of granola, and ¼ cup of mixed berries.
2. Repeat the layers.
3. Optional: Drizzle with honey.

Nutrition facts:
(per serving)

Calories: 490cals
Carbs: 40g
Protein: 20g
Fat: 10g

What do you call cheese that isn't yours?

Nacho cheese!

Turkey Cream Cheese Wraps

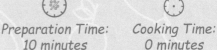

Preparation Time:
10 minutes

Cooking Time:
0 minutes

Servings:
1

Ingredients:

- 1 Whole Wheat Tortilla
- 2 tablespoons Chive and Onion Cream Cheese spread
- 3 slices Deli Turkey
- 6 slices Cucumber (thinly sliced)
- 1 leaf Green Leaf Lettuce, or shredded Lettuce
- 1 Toothpick (Optional)

Nutrition facts:
(per serving)

- Calories: 320cals
- Carbs: 31g
- Protein: 11g
- Fat: 18g

Instructions:

1. Spread the tortilla with cream cheese, leaving a 1-inch border.
2. Arrange turkey and vegetables down the middle of the wrap.
3. Roll up, and secure with a toothpick (optional).
4. If desired, grill the wrap briefly in a skillet, pressing down lightly.
5. Grill until the tortilla is golden brown and crisp.

Sandwich Kabobs

Preparation Time:
10 minutes

Cooking Time:
0 minutes

Servings:
4

Ingredients:

- 4 slices Bread
- Cheddar Cheese Block (firm)
- Turkey or Ham, sliced
- 8 Cherry Tomatoes
- Handful of Lettuce Leaves

You will also need:
- Wooden Skewers
- Small Cookie Cutters

Nutrition facts:
(per serving)

Calories: 170cals
Carbs: 10g
Protein: 12g
Fat: 10g

Instructions:

1. Using the cookie cutters, cut your bread and cheese into desired shapes.
2. Cut cheese slices thick enough to accommodate the width of your cookie cutter.
3. Slice the large cheese slices in half.
4. Using cookie cutters, cut shapes out of cheese chunks and bread.
5. Layer the ingredients however you desire on the skewers.
6. Enjoy your sandwich kabob!

What do you call cheese that isn't yours?

Nacho cheese!

No Cook Pizza

Ingredients:

- 2 English Muffins or Pita Bread, sliced horizontally
- ½ cup Tomato Sauce
- 1 cup Shredded Cheese
- ½ cup Mini Pepperoni slices
- ¼ cup Sliced Olives
- Baby Spinach (Optional for fun face)
- Bell Peppers (Optional for fun face)

Nutrition facts:
(per serving)

Calories: 330cals
Carbs: 30g
Protein: 40g
Fat: 15g

Instructions:

1. Spread ¼ cup of tomato sauce on each English muffin or pita bread.
2. Sprinkle ½ cup of shredded cheese on top.
3. Add ¼ cup of mini pepperoni slices and 1 tablespoon of sliced olives on each.
4. You can make fun faces using olives as eyes, nose, red bell peppers as eyebrows, baby spinach as hairs.

What do you call a fake noodle?

An impasta!

36

Mr Octopus Sandwich

Ingredients:

- 2 slices Whole Wheat Bread
- 1 Lettuce Leaf
- 1 Scrambled Egg
- 2 Radish slices
- 2 Olive
- 1 Cucumber slice
- 8 red pepper , thinly sliced

Nutrition facts:
(per serving)
Calories: 180cals
Carbs: 17g
Protein: 11g
Fat: 8g

Instructions:

1. Scramble eggs and cook them until they're fluffy.
2. Take two round slices of whole wheat bread.
3. Place lettuce on one roundel.
4. Spread the scrambled eggs over the lettuce.
5. Cover it with the other bread slice.
6. Add radish slices for eyes on top of the bread slice.
7. Use olives as pupils for the radish eyes.
8. Create a smiling mouth using cucumber slices.
9. Attach eight red pepper strips to the bottom of the sandwich, spreading them out to resemble tentacles.

Easter Bunny

Ingredients:

- 1 slice of Green Apple
- Half a Banana
- 1 Baby Carrot
- 1 Raspberry
- 2 Blueberries

Instructions:

1. Grab your slice of green apple and place it on a plate, towards the bottom.
2. Take your 2 blueberries and place them on the apple slice to make eyes. Then grab your red raspberry and place it on the apple slice for a nose.
3. Using your knife, slice your baby carrot into 6 thin strips. Place these thin strips beside the raspberry nose for whiskers – 3 on each side.
4. Finally, using your knife, slice your banana in half lengthwise. Place these 2 halves on top of the apple slice for bunny ears.

Nutrition facts:
(per serving)

- Calories: 60cals
- Carbs: 4g
- Protein: 2g
- Fat: 1g

What did one plate say to another plate?

Tonight, dinner's on me!

Ants on a Log

Ingredients:

- 4 Celery Stalks
- ½ cup Peanut Butter or Nut Butter (approximately)
- ¼ cup Raisins (approximately)
- 7-8 Green Grapes (Optional topping)
- 7-8 Red Grapes (Optional topping)
- 1 Apple slice (Optional topping)
- 1 Orange slice (Optional topping)
- 1 Cucumber slice (Optional topping)

Nutrition facts:
(per serving)

Calories: 150cals
Carbs: 9g
Protein: 6g
Fat: 7g

Instructions:

1. Cut the celery stalks into smaller pieces, each about 3 inches long.
2. Spread peanut butter or nut butter inside each celery piece.
3. Place approximately 1 tablespoon of raisins on top of the peanut butter or nut butter in each celery piece to create "ants on a log."
4. Add your any favorite optional topping on top of the peanut butter or nut butter.

Why don't elephants use computers?

Because they're afraid of the mouse!

What do you call a bee that can't make up its mind?

A maybee!

SNACKS

Apple Nachos

Ingredients:

- 2 Apples, cored and sliced
- ¼ cup Peanut Butter or Nut Butter
- 2 tablespoons Chocolate Chips
- 2 tablespoons Shredded Coconut
- Colorful Sprinkles (Optional topping)

Instructions:

1. Arrange apple slices on a plate.
2. Spread peanut butter or nut butter on top of apple slices.
3. Sprinkle chocolate chips and shredded coconut on top.
4. Add colorful sprinkles on top.

Nutrition facts:
(per serving)
- Calories: 50cals
- Carbs: 5g
- Protein: 3g
- Fat: 4g

What's a ghost's favorite dessert?

Boo-berry pie!

Trail Mix Cups

Ingredients:

- 1 cup Granola
- ½ cup Mixed Nuts
- ¼ cup Dried Fruits (Raisins, Cranberries)
- ¼ cup Chocolate Chips

Instructions:

1. Mix granola, nuts, dried fruits, and chocolate chips in a bowl.
2. Portion into small cups for easy snacking.

Nutrition facts:
(per serving)

Calories: 250cals
Carbs: 30g
Protein: 12g
Fat: 10g

What's a pirate's favorite letter?

Arrrrrr!

Veggie Cups with Dip

Preparation Time: 15 minutes

Cooking Time: 0 minutes

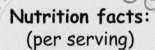

Servings: 4

Ingredients:

- 1 cup Baby Carrots
- 1 cup Cucumber Sticks
- 1 cup Cherry Tomatoes
- ½ cup Hummus for dipping

Instructions:

1. Arrange 1 cup of baby carrots, 1 cup of cucumber sticks, and 1 cup of cherry tomatoes in cups.
2. Serve with approximately ½ cup of hummus for dipping.

Nutrition facts:
(per serving)
- Calories: 66cals
- Carbs: 4g
- Protein: 4g
- Fat: 6g

What's a skeleton's least favorite room in the house?

The living room!

44

Honey Banana Sushi Rolls

Preparation Time: 15 minutes

Cooking Time: 0 minutes

Servings: 2

Ingredients:

- 2 Tortillas
- 2 tablespoons Peanut Butter or Nut Butter (approximately)
- 2 Bananas
- Honey for drizzling
- Colorful Cereal or Nuts (Optional)

Nutrition facts:
(per serving)

Calories: 440cals
Carbs: 39g
Protein: 21g
Fat: 19g

Instructions:

1. Spread approximately 1 tablespoon of peanut butter or nut butter on each tortilla.
2. Place one banana in the center of each tortilla.
3. Drizzle with honey according to your preference.
4. Roll up the tortillas.
5. Add honey outside of tortilla and sprinkle any cereal or nuts on it.
6. Eat whole, or slice into sushi bites.

Why did the cow go to outer space?

To see the moooon!

Chia Seed Protein Bites with Nuts

Preparation Time: 15 minutes

Cooking Time: 0 minutes

Servings: 2

Ingredients:

- 1 ½ cups Quick-cooking Oats
- ½ cup Almond butter or Creamy Peanut Butter or Nut Butter
- ½ cup Chia Seeds
- ½ cup Honey
- ¼ cup Vanilla or Chocolate Protein Powder
- ¼ cup unsweetened Shredded Coconut
- Additional unsweetened Shredded Coconut, optional
- Handful of Chopped Nuts (Walnuts, Almonds etc)

Nutrition facts:
(per serving)
- Calories: 80cals
- Carbs: 5g
- Protein: 4g
- Fat: 5g

Instructions:

1. In a large bowl, combine the first 6 ingredients.
2. Refrigerate 1 hour or until firm enough to roll.
3. Shape into 1- ½ -in. balls.
4. Roll in chopped nuts and additional coconut if desired.
5. Store in the refrigerator.

Why did the chicken join a band?

Because it had the drumsticks!

No-Bake Oatmeal Cookies

Preparation Time:
15 minutes

Cooking Time:
0 minutes

Servings:
6

Ingredients:

- 1 cup Rolled oats
- ½ cup Peanut Butter or Nut Butter
- 1/3 cup Honey
- ½ cup Chocolate Chips
- 1 teaspoon Vanilla Extract
- M&Ms (Optional topping)

Nutrition facts:
(per serving)

Calories: 30cals
Carbs: 10g
Protein: 0g
Fat: 0g

Instructions:

1. Mix rolled oats, peanut butter or nut butter, honey, chocolate chips, and vanilla extract in a bowl.
2. Scoop spoonfuls onto a lined tray and refrigerate until set.
3. After it gets set add optional topping of your choice on it.

How do you organize a space party?

You planet!

47

Fruity Yogurt Cones

Preparation Time:
10 minutes

Cooking Time:
0 minutes

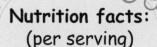

Servings:
4

Ingredients:

- 4 Waffle Cones
- 1 cup Vanilla Yogurt
- 1 cup sliced Strawberries
- ½ cup Blueberries

Instructions:

1. Fill each waffle cone with approximately ¼ cup of vanilla yogurt.
2. Top each cone with approximately ¼ cup of sliced strawberries and 2 tablespoons of blueberries.

Nutrition facts:
(per serving)

» Calories: 51cals
» Carbs: 7g
» Protein: 1g
» Fat: 4g

How do you catch a squirrel?

Climb a tree and act like a nut!

Fruity Fun Skewers

Preparation Time: 15 minutes

Cooking Time: 0 minutes

Servings: 5

Ingredients:

- 5 Large Strawberries, halved
- Few Berries (Blueberries, Raspberries and Cherries)
- $\frac{1}{4}$ Cantaloupe, cut into small cubes
- 5 – 6 Pineapple Chunks
- 2 sliced Kiwi
- 10 Skewers

Nutrition facts:
(per serving)
Calories: 60cals
Carbs: 15g
Protein: 1g
Fat: 0g

Instructions:

1. Thread strawberries, cantaloupe, raspberries, blueberries, pineapple, kiwi and cherries alternately onto skewers.
2. Arrange skewers decoratively on a serving platter.

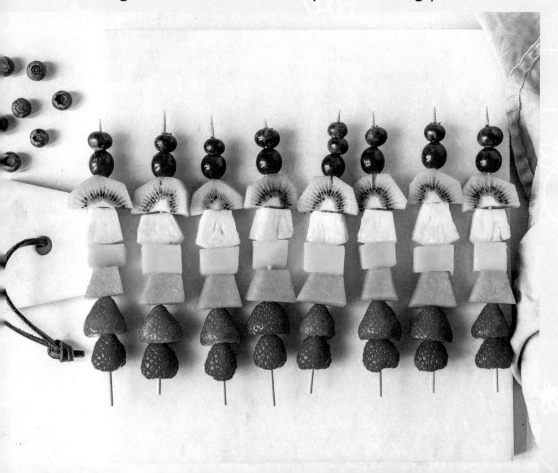

Animal Crackers

Preparation Time: 30 minutes

Cooking Time: 10 minutes

Servings: 24

Ingredients:

- ½ cup Rolled Oats
- ¾ cup All-purpose Flour
- ¼ teaspoon Baking Soda
- ¼ teaspoon Salt
- ¼ cup Butter
- 2 teaspoons Honey
- ¼ cup Buttermilk

Nutrition facts:
(per serving)

» Calories: 50cals
» Carbs: 5g
» Protein: 3g
» Fat: 2g

Instructions:

1. Preheat the oven to 400 degrees F (200 degrees C). Grind oats until fine using a blender or food processor.
2. In a medium bowl, stir together the blended oats, flour, baking soda and salt. Cut in the butter using a pastry blender or your fingers until the butter lumps are smaller than peas.
3. Stir in the buttermilk and honey to form a stiff dough. On a lightly floured surface, roll the dough out to 1/8 inch in thickness.
4. Cut into desired shapes with cookie cutters. Place cookies 1 inch apart onto cookie sheets.
5. Bake for 5 to 7 minutes in the preheated oven, until the edges are lightly browned.
6. Remove from cookie sheets to cool on wire racks.

Peanut Butter or Nut Butter Banana Bites

Preparation Time: 10 minutes

Cooking Time: 0 minutes

Servings: 3

Ingredients:

- 1 Banana, sliced
- 1 tablespoon Peanut Butter or Nut Butter
- Honey for drizzling
- Mini Chocolate Chips (Optional)

Instructions:

1. Spread a small amount of peanut butter or nut butter on each banana slice.
2. Drizzle honey on it.
3. Optionally, Sprinkle mini chocolate chips on top.

Nutrition facts:
(per serving)

Calories: 121cals
Carbs: 25g
Protein: 3g
Fat: 4g

What did one wall say to the other wall?

"I'll meet you at the corner!"

What did one ocean say to the other ocean?

Nothing, they just waved!

Why do birds fly south for the winter?

Because it's too far to walk!

DESSERTS

Frozen Yogurt Bark

Preparation Time:
15 minutes

Cooking Time:
0 minutes

Servings:
7

Ingredients:

- 2 cups Greek Yogurt
- 2 tablespoons Honey
- Assorted Berries (Blueberries, Strawberries)
- Granola
- Popsicle Sticks

Nutrition facts:
(per serving)

» Calories: 50cals
» Carbs: 6g
» Protein: 2g
» Fat: 1g

Instructions:

1. Mix Greek yogurt and honey.
2. Spread the mixture on an ice cube tray.
3. You can place popsicles stick inside it.
4. Sprinkle berries and granola on top.
5. Freeze until solid and unmold it after.

Chocolate Covered Banana Pops

Ingredients:

- 2 Bananas, peeled and cut in half
- ½ cup Chocolate Chips
- Assorted Toppings (shredded coconut, chopped nuts, sprinkles)
- 4 Popsicle Sticks

Instructions:

1. Insert a popsicle stick into each banana half.
2. Melt chocolate chips in a microwave-safe bowl.
3. Dip each banana into the melted chocolate.
4. Roll in toppings of your choice.
5. Place on parchment paper to set.

Nutrition facts:
(per serving)

Calories: 350cals
Carbs: 28g
Protein: 6g
Fat: 17g

Why did the bicycle fall over?

It was two-tired!

Rainbow Jello Cups

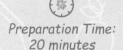

Preparation Time: 20 minutes

Cooking Time: 0 minutes

Servings: 2

Ingredients:

- Various colors/flavors of Jello
- Whipped Cream
- Jellies (Optional)

Instructions:

1. Prepare each color/flavor of Jello according to package instructions.
2. Allow each layer to set before adding the next.
3. Once all layers are set top it with whipped cream.
4. You can add jellies on top for decoration.

Nutrition facts:
(per serving)
- Calories: 124cals
- Carbs: 29g
- Protein: 2g
- Fat: 1g

What do you call a bear that's stuck in the rain?

A drizzly bear!

Banana Ice cream

Preparation Time: 15 minutes

Cooking Time: 0 minutes

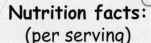

Servings: 2

Ingredients:

- 3 ripe Bananas, frozen
- 2 tablespoons Cocoa Powder
- $\frac{1}{4}$ cup Milk (optional)

Instructions:

1. Blend frozen bananas until creamy.
2. Add cocoa powder and blend until combined.
3. Add milk if a smoother consistency is desired.
4. Scoop into bowls, serve sliced banana with it, and enjoy.

Nutrition facts:
(per serving)

Calories: 180cals
Carbs: 32g
Protein: 5g
Fat: 5g

What do you call a shoe made of a banana?

A slipper!

Fairy Cream Bread

Preparation Time: 15 minutes

Cooking Time: 0 minutes

Servings: 3

Ingredients:

- 3 White Bread slice
- 3 oz of Cream Cheese, Butter, or Margarin
- 2 tablespoons of Sugar
- Rainbow Sprinkles

Instructions:

1. Mix the cream cheese and sugar.
2. Cut the crust off of the bread.
3. Using a rolling pin, roll the square bread pieces until they are thin.
4. Place a thin layer of the sugary cream cheese on top of the square bread
5. Pour rainbow sprinkles on top (believe it or not, kids are really great at this)
6. Take the sprinkled bread and roll it into a slightly tight spiral shape.

Nutrition facts:
(per serving)

- Calories: 181cals
- Carbs: 29g
- Protein: 3g
- Fat: 7g

Why don't skeletons fight each other?

They don't have the guts!

Strawberry Nutella Pizza

Preparation Time: 10 minutes

Cooking Time: 12 minutes

Servings: 8

Ingredients:

- Ready made Pizza Crust (Optional: 1 lb. Pizza Dough)
- ½ tablespoon Butter melted
- 4-5 tablespoons Nutella
- ½ cup Strawberries sliced
- ¼ cup White Chocolate Chips

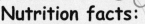

Nutrition facts:
(per serving)

Calories: 310cals
Carbs: 24g
Protein: 5g
Fat: 13g

Instructions:

1. Place ready made pizza crust on pizza pan.
2. Optional: Prepare Pizza dough as directed on package, cool 10 min.
3. Spread Nutella evenly over crust.
4. On top of the Nutella, add your sliced strawberries and white chocolate chips.
5. Using a pizza cutter, slice into triangle pieces and enjoy!

What did one hat say to the other?

Stay here, I'm going on ahead!

No-Bake Energy Bites

Preparation Time:
15 minutes

Cooking Time:
0 minutes

Servings:
3

Ingredients:

- 1 cup Rolled Oats
- ½ cup Peanut Butter or Nut Butter
- 1/3 cup Honey
- 1 cup Shredded Coconut
- ½ cup Mini Chocolate Chips
- 1 teaspoon Vanilla Extract

Instructions:

1. In a bowl, mix rolled oats, peanut butter or nut butter, honey, shredded coconut, mini chocolate chips, and vanilla extract.
2. Refrigerate the mixture for 30 minutes.
3. Roll the mixture into small bites.
4. Store in the refrigerator until ready to serve.

Nutrition facts:
(per serving)
- Calories: 160cals
- Carbs: 15g
- Protein: 9g
- Fat: 4g

What do you call a pile of cats?

A meowtain!

Chocolate Covered Pretzel Rods

Preparation Time: 15 minutes

Cooking Time: 10 minutes

Servings: 6

Ingredients:

- 12 Pretzel Rods
- 1 cup Milk Chocolate Chips
- Assorted toppings (Sprinkles, Crushed Nuts)

Nutrition facts:
(per serving)

Calories: 150cals
Carbs: 15g
Protein: 6g
Fat: 6g

Instructions:

1. Melt 1 cup of milk chocolate chips in the microwave or using a double boiler.
2. Dip each pretzel rod into the melted chocolate, covering them halfway.
3. Roll the chocolate-covered pretzels in assorted toppings such as sprinkles or crushed nuts.
4. Place the chocolate-covered pretzels on a parchment-lined tray.
5. Allow the chocolate to set.
6. Enjoy these delightful Chocolate Covered Pretzel Rods!

Oreo Dirt Cup

Ingredients:

- 2 cups Cold Milk
- 1 (3.9-ounce) package Instant Chocolate Pudding (4 serving size)
- 8 ounces Frozen Whipped Topping, thawed
- 1 ½ cups crushed Chocolate Sandwich Cookies (about 16), divided
- 20 Gummy Worms

Nutrition facts:
(per serving)
- Calories: 280cals
- Carbs: 45g
- Protein: 3g
- Fat: 11g

Instructions:

1. Whisk together milk and instant pudding for 2 minutes, until pudding is completely dissolved. Let stand 5 minutes to thicken.
2. Stir in frozen whipped topping and ½ cup of crushed cookies.
3. Spoon into 10 individual cups.
4. Sprinkle remaining crushed cookies over pudding mixture. Top each cup with 2 gummy worms.
5. Chill for at least 60 minutes or until ready to serve.

Mini Fruit Tarts

Preparation Time:
15 minutes

Cooking Time:
0 minutes

Servings:
6

Ingredients:

- 12 Mini Tart Shells (store-bought or homemade)
- 1 cup Vanilla Pudding
- Assorted Fresh Fruits (e.g., 1 cup of Berries, 2 Kiwis, etc.)
- $\frac{1}{4}$ cup Apricot Jam (for glaze)

Instructions:

1. Fill each mini tart shell with approximately 1 tablespoon of vanilla pudding.
2. Top the vanilla puddings with assorted fresh fruits. Adjust the quantity based on your preference.
3. Heat $\frac{1}{4}$ cup of apricot jam until it becomes liquid. Brush the liquid apricot jam over the fresh fruits for a shiny glaze.
4. Chill the mini fruit tarts in the refrigerator before serving.

Nutrition facts:
(per serving)

Calories: 149cals
Carbs: 26g
Protein: 14g
Fat: 10g

What did one plate say to another plate?

Lunch is on me!

Made in United States
Troutdale, OR
04/11/2024